Uprising

How the Yellow Vest Protests are Changing
France and Overturning the World Order

STEPHEN R. TURLEY, PH.D.

A New Conservative Age is Rising
www.TurleyTalks.com

Table of Contents

Paris is Burning: The Fall of the Globalist World Order

It all seemed to start as a protest against escalating gasoline taxes. That's at least what the media largely reported in November of 2018, as massive crowds began to assemble in France's cities. But it didn't take long to recognize that something far surpassing any particular tax or regulation was surfacing on the streets of Paris, Marseille, Metz, Nice, Bordeaux, and in Toulouse. Indeed, protestors wearing the characteristic 'yellow vest' began spilling over into Brussels, Portugal, the Netherlands, the UK, and even Canada. It soon became apparent that this was no mere protest; this was the makings of a worldwide uprising.

At the time of this writing, for nearly five months, what has been called the Yellow Vest Uprising has dominated the political scene within France and has effectively crippled the Macron presidency. Thus far, there have been 11 recorded fatalities, and, according to the newspaper, Libération, 109 protesters have been seriously injured, including 18 who have become blind in one eye and four who have lost a hand.[1] Needless to say, there have been thousands of arrests, and Paris has been a mess with graffiti-scrawled over monuments and shattered glass and burned cars. The Uprising is without question an absolute wildfire that has grown beyond the containing capacities of police authorities, who have often relied on counter-measures of escalating violence, which has only seemed to fuel the anger and the resentment.

As for Macron himself, the Yellow Vest Uprising has been a political disaster. Even before the Uprising, only about 25 percent of the population approved of his leadership, while 71 percent said they had no confidence in him at all. But as soon as the protests reached their second and third weeks, Macron's approval rating dipped to an embarrassing 18 percent. Things had become so bad that Newsweek headlined their coverage of the demonstrations with the question: "Will Macron survive?"

But that question has been increasingly eclipsed by the far larger question that more and more pundits are asking: *Will the globalist political order survive*? As each week goes by marked by renewed protests, more journalists and scholars are beginning to realize that the Yellow Vest Uprising poses nothing less than perhaps the single greatest threat to the

---

[1]https://www.nytimes.com/2019/01/28/world/europe/france-yellow-vests-police.html.

globalist world order that we have yet seen. I was particularly struck by an article on the Australian site Adelaide.com written by contributor Andrew Hunter, who makes a very interesting argument: he notices quite rightly that the Yellow Vest Uprising is emphatically *not* a partisan movement. It's not representing any particular party or political platform or policy. In fact, the Yellow Vest Uprising has nothing to do with any political cooperation at all, and therein is the whole point! The protestors simply don't believe that any solution to their economic and cultural predicaments can be found in the current structures and its elected representatives, and *this* is why the Yellow Vest Uprising is such an existential threat to the globalist world order. What makes the Yellow Vest Uprising so dangerous to the current world order is that their unrelenting demands *find virtually no possible solution within the given globalist structures and its representative elite.*

For example, if we were to draw parallels between the Yellow Vests and say the Popular Front uprising in the 1930s, we would immediately notice that the Popular Front identified with the political leftwing; they self-consciously aligned themselves with the French Communist Party, Workers International, and the Radical and Socialist Party. As such, the Popular Front was responding to their contemporary problems by advocating solutions provided by their current political structure. This is simply not the case with the Yellow Vest Uprising. They've rejected an alliance with any established French political party; it appears that most of its participants either didn't vote in the last presidential election, or they voted for Le Pen and the National Rally. Given that a majority of French citizens approve of the protests and the cause for which they stand, and given that these demonstrations have spread throughout Europe and even into Canada, we may, in fact, be looking at that movement that finally hits at the heart of globalist establishments so as to bring them down once and for all, which for Hunter means the end of liberal democracy and liberal democratic institutions.

Now, let me note where I think Hunter goes awry in his analysis. Hunter rather carelessly asserts that the Yellow Vest Uprising poses a very dire warning for what he calls 'democracies.' By 'democracies,' it is rather clear throughout the article that he's referring to the particular *kind* of democracy that is allowed – indeed that's mandated – by globalization, and hence, by implication, he's talking about a dire warning for globalization itself. However, populist movements such as the Yellow Vests are emphatically *not* anti-democratic; the data is in on this, and it's unfortunate that it seems that Hunter has not availed himself of these studies. What these studies have demonstrated is that populists are not against democracy itself; in 2017, Pew Research found across Europe and the United States that an average of 90 percent of their populations saw democracy as a good way of governing their countries. And a World

Values Survey found the same totals.[2] The super-majority of Europeans, which other studies have found to include at least 25 to 30 percent committed nationalist populists, feel very, very good about democracy. Democracy isn't going anywhere.

What nationalist populists are very concerned about are certain *aspects* of democracy, which is fundamentally different than being opposed to democracy itself. In fact, as Eatwell and Goodwin have documented, far from being anti-democratic, national populist voters want *more* democracy; they want *more* referendums, and they want *more* politicians who are actually going to listen to their concerns and who will, in turn, give *more* power to the people and less power to established economic and political elites.[3] Nationalist populists are far more interested in 'direct democracy' rather than the kind that derives from Brussels which so often overrides the concerns of the populations of sovereign nations.

To help clarify this point, Eatwell and Goodwin's recent study on the nationalist populist movement makes a distinction between what they call 'redemptive' democracy and 'pragmatic' democracy.[4] The kind of democracy that operates within globalist world structures is a highly pragmatic democracy; it's based on the 'pragmatism' of the

---

[2] Roger Eatwell and Matthew Goodwin, *National Populism: The Revolt Against Liberal Democracy* (London: Pelican Books, 2018), 116-117.
[3] Ibid.
[4] Ibid, 48.

technocratic expertise of a ruling elite whose values are often fundamentally different from that of the people. By contrast, populists are for what we might call a redemptive vision of democracy, which restores democratic rule and institutions as compatible with the values of the population which protects the rights of citizens, as well as the nation's culture, customs, and traditions, and seeks to rid the nation as much as possible of corrupt and distant political elites. This is the whole notion of democracy that is animating and inspiring the nationalist populist movements throughout Europe, and most especially, the Yellow Vest Uprising.

And so, while democracy is safe and sound, the world order comprised of the pragmatism of the economic and political elites is most definitely in mortal danger. The Yellow Vest Uprising, which shows no signs of faltering any time soon and whose influence is spreading way beyond France, does indeed appear to be one of the single greatest threats to the globalist world order that we've seen thus far. In what follows, I want to explore this threat. I begin by further underscoring the dire straits that the globalist liberal order is currently in, of which the Yellow Vest Uprising is a particularly poignant indicator. In Chapter 2, I look at the Yellow Vest movement itself, analyzing the deeply profound symbolism of the yellow vest and how it functions within the movement. Chapter 3 considers why French President Macron's attempts to quell the Uprising will not work long term, and Chapter 4 briefly surveys four ways in which the Uprising has effectively changed France. Chapter

5 will look at the prospects for the emergence of a New French Right, while Chapter 6 considers how the Uprising is influencing an eventual nationalist takeover of Europe.

It is my hope that by exploring these various dimensions of the Yellow Vest Uprising, we will better appreciate this profound social movement and how it indicates wider political, economic, and cultural dynamics that extend far beyond France and that are indeed, changing the world.

CHAPTER ONE

The End of the Inevitability of Globalism

Rodger Baker, a strategic analyst for the Stratfor Institute, recently published a very interesting article that echoes the sentiments of a growing number of scholars: the utopian visions of a globalist world order dreamt up by many of our political and economic elite is indeed beginning to collapse.[5] Though the Startfor report does not mention him by name, it's rather clear that the main intellectual force that the report is rebutting is the famed political scientist, Francis Fukuyama and his 'end of history' thesis. A couple of decades back, Fukuyama put forward a bold thesis that argued that with the defeat of fascism in World War II and the collapse of communism and the end the Cold War, the history of political and social order had evolved finally into the triumph of liberal

---

[5] https://worldview.stratfor.com/article/challenging-inevitability-liberal-world-order.

democracies around the world.[6] As such, the world had finally arrived through this long historical process to discover the single best political and economic system for all peoples around the globe. It was a highly influential thesis among neo-liberals. In many ways, theorists and politicians, echoing Fukuyama, believed that it was the European Union that was the supposed apex of this historical progression with its combination of democratic institutions, integrated markets, and open borders. This is what Fukuyama now infamously referred to as the 'end of history,' a global liberal democratic order that would usher in an era of peace and prosperity around the world.

Well, as it turns out, Fukuyama later published a piece entitled 'Second Thoughts.'[7] However, in many respects, the intellectual and ideological damage had already been done, and bureaucrats, eurocrats, theorists, pundits, and media-types all began to operate from the vantage point of not merely the inevitability of the triumph of liberal globalization, but actually began to openly excoriate, disparage and indeed censor any and all who took issue with such a thesis, either theoretically or politically.

But now, scholars and theorists are themselves beginning to have second thoughts. For example, Larry Diamond, an expert on democratic societies, found that between 2000

---

[6]https://www.embl.de/aboutus/science_society/discussion/discussion_ 2006/ref1-22june06.pdf.
[7]https://www.embl.de/aboutus/science_society/discussion/discussion_ 2006/ref2-22june06.pdf.

and 2015, nearly 30 liberal democracies around the world collapsed, and this did not take into account the most recent example in Turkey under the presidency of Recep Tayyip Erdoğan. As attempts to impose liberal democracy on the Middle East have demonstrated, their version of a democratic society looks nothing like what the West envisioned for it. And with President Trump's preparation for mass withdrawals of U.S. troops from the region, it does appear that nation-building in the image of Western liberal democracy has come to an end.

Baker summarizes well the root of this collapse:

> At its most extreme, the liberal world order, whether represented by EU leaders in Brussels, the World Trade Organization or even the United Nations, denotes the subservience of national and regional self-interest to a rules-based global order that assumes a universality of application and applicability. Commendably, it attempts to relegate conflict and competition to the dustbin of history, but it does so by ignoring certain underlying truths: That place matters, that opportunity is not equally bestowed by nature across the globe and that — for good or bad — societies, morals and norms evolved differently in different places as organized people interacted with their local geographies.

Baker goes on to note that the near religious zeal for a universalist and inevitable principle of world organization, that is, of course, known today as globalization, is hardly new in human history. We saw the Babylonian version, the Persian version, the Greek version, the Roman version, the Byzantine and Holy Roman Empire versions, the Enlightenment version, the colonialist version. The word we generally use for such aspirations is 'imperialism,' and globalization, as much as its erudite proponents want to squirm away from such characterization, is fully compatible with such aspirations. Globalization is and always will be an imperial world system that seeks to impose its will on nations and regions that want nothing to do with it. Hence, we have this massive backlash all over the world in the form of a renewed sense of nation, culture, custom, and tradition as mechanisms of resistance against the colonizing dynamics of globalization and its secular aristocracy.

Now interestingly, we see this clash, this dialectic, between the globalist and the nationalist even domestically, at a micro level as it were. Most Western nations are turning into an urban/rural dialectic, where capital and finance are relocating around mass metropolitan centers, leaving rural areas largely disenfranchised from this economic recalibration. Given the relocation of finance around urban areas, Baker notes that globalization still remains a high ideal among urban populations in the West; when you go to the cosmopolitan centers such as Brussels, Berlin, London, New York, Los Angles, you will find there still a highly idealized notion of the full integration of political protocols, trade flows, and financial structures that, we might say, can distract cosmopolitans from the reality of the collapse of globalism that is going on all around them.

And as it turns out, the collapse of globalism has indeed come right into the heart of the urban area, particularly with the Yellow Vest Uprising, which, in many respects, is the revolt of the rural. This is because globalization has created something that scholars call a global division of labor, where manufacturing and industrial factory jobs are shipped out to third world nations while capital and finance are relocated to urban centers, and this process has left rural populations highly unemployed. So French citizens living in rural areas have seen their manufacturing jobs vanish, being shipped overseas, and, therefore, can only find work in cities like Paris. But they do not have the money to live in Paris because of its gentrification; all the high-paying finance jobs that have dominated the cities of late have driven up the cost of living there. They do not have jobs where they live, and they cannot live where there are jobs. They have to commute, sometimes very long distances; and then, President Macron turns around and has the insulting gall to slap a massive fuel tax on these rural workers. Needless to say, they rightly blew up, and they're still blowing up because they, the Yellow Vest protestors, recognize that there simply is no solution within the current governing political order. They are not just looking for Macron's resignation but indeed the resignation of the entire dominant globalist order as well. That is why scholars and pundits are coming out and saying that the

Yellow Vest Uprising is indeed a threat to the entire globalist order.

Baker ends his piece by recommending a very different course of action from this point forward. The vision of an inevitable globalized world order for all practical purposes is dead, and the whole irony to this is that if Western leaders want to begin quelling the rise of these supposedly dangerous nationalist populist movements going on all over the world, they are going to first have to quell their own globalist sentiments and resign themselves to the fact that a return to nation, culture, custom, and tradition is indeed the dominant political order for the foreseeable future.

CHAPTER TWO

The Symbolic Power of the Yellow Vest

Among the number of articles written on the Yellow Vest Uprising, one of the more interesting and insightful pieces was by Vanessa Friedman of *The New York Times* who focused on the extraordinary power of the visual symbolism of the yellow vest.[8] She notes that the high-visibility characteristic of the garment is, in fact, an ingenious modern uniform of rebellion. For example, note that the yellow vest was designed by its very nature to be seen, recognized, and noticed in the particular case of roadside and vehicular safety; this was an especially ingenious move on the part of the protestors. The yellow vest by its design is supposed to catch people's attention; it's immediately recognizable, impossible to miss even on the small screens of social media. Moreover, it's easy to slip

---

[8] https://www.nytimes.com/2018/12/04/fashion/yellow-vests-france-protest-fashion.html.

over any outfit, and it's instantly transformative, and, perhaps most profoundly, it is universally understood as a distress signal! The yellow vest is universally understood as indicating that something has broken down and is in need of rescue and repair.

Furthermore, the yellow vest is a symbol of the working class, such as those involved in construction; and yet, it's also universal, in the sense that all French motorists are supposed to keep a high-visibility garment in their cars in case of problems, so everyone owns one. Friedman points out that the yellow vest is so accessible that it can seem to include even those who are actually not taking part in the movement. A particularly humorous example was when President Macron landed in Argentina for the G-20 summit, shortly after the Yellow Vest Uprising began, and was first greeted on the tarmac by airport workers wearing yellow vests! Twitter couldn't help lighting up with pictures, memes, and tweets pointing out the irony.

Friedman rightly goes on to point out that dress is an extremely important cultural signifier. We can all intuit that as a matter of common sense, but scholars have long recognized the importance of clothing as a cultural and social signifier. The scholar, Grant David McCracken has done a lot of work in this area, and he's concluded that clothing is a powerful means by which cultural categories and principles are encoded on our bodies.[9] Clothing is an extraordinary signifier of identity and not just our personal identities; our clothing inevitably reflects collective and cultural identities. When we dress a certain way, we are identifying with the culture which that dress substantiates and embodies. This is why wedding dresses or graduation gowns and the like or so powerful; clothing signifies identities that transcend our own and are, therefore, a powerful means by which our own identities are transformed.

And this is particularly important with the Yellow Vest Uprising, especially given that it is thus far a highly decentralized movement; it hasn't aligned with any particular political party, though it does appear to be moving solidly in favor of the nationalist populist right as represented by Marine Le Pen's National Rally. Nevertheless, the Yellow Vests are not formally aligned with any political party or platform; the movement has no centralized organization or leadership; and so the decentralized nature of the Yellow Vest movement means that the yellow vests themselves are even more important as a unifying thread and call to arms, as the author puts it in the article. And so, the Yellow Vest Uprising is a further instance that demonstrates what scholars have long observed, that the body in many respects is the primary agency for cultural production since we all relate to ourselves and others in and through bodies. And as

---

[9] See, for example, Grant McCracken, *Transformations: Identity Construction in Contemporary Culture* (Bloomington: Indiana University Press, 2008).

those bodies are, of course, clothed, the clothing becomes a powerful signifier of not only my own identity but my own identity *within* a particular culture or people group.

In addition to the yellow vest uniform, perhaps one of the most interesting developments within the Uprising is an emerging Christian symbolism that's serving to further unify the movement.[10] If you look closely at pictures of the yellow vest garments, you'll see symbols and phrases marked on them such as the Latin 'DEUS VULT,' which means 'God wills it' or 'God willing,' a well-known rallying cry among the Crusaders. There are images of the Virgin Mary, particularly with tears coming out of her eyes, drawn on a number of yellow vests. You'll see the phrase 'Babylon on fire' spray painted on buildings. Indeed, many of the French flags waved during the protests have the Cross of Lorraine, which is a symbol of French patriotism and a liberated France, particularly as it recalls its use in the 19th century as a rallying point for the French to recover its lost provinces; the flag was also used as a rallying point during WWII against Nazi occupation.

As commentators have noted, the Yellow Vests are looking for a language and a symbolism that unites them in what appears increasingly to be a meaningless time, when billboards seem to speak to us more than religious icons; when a nation's culture, customs, and traditions appear to

---

[10] https://cruxnow.com/church-in-europe/2019/03/16/christian-symbols-enter-frances-yellow-vest-demonstrations/.

be more and more negated and eclipsed by globalist-driven consumerism and standardized political and economic systems that are radically impersonal and indeed de-personalizing. As such, the increasing use of Christian symbolism among the Yellow Vests is an indicator of what scholars call *retraditionalization*. In the face of anti-cultural threats posed by globalized dynamics, scholars have noticed among populations a renewed interest in "traditions of wisdom that have proved their validity through the test of history," or "a longing for spiritual traditions and practices that have stood the test of time, and, therefore, can be valued as authentic resources for spiritual renewal."[11] The important point here is that retraditionalization is not limited simply to spiritual renewal or religious revival; it often involves a reconfiguration of political, cultural, and educational norms around pre-modern religious beliefs and practices as a response to the secularizing processes of globalization.[12]

Because globalization sees each particular culture and custom as impediments to political and economic standardization, globalized processes have a tendency to (at best) marginalize or (at worst) eradicate the cultural and traditional customs, practices and identities of individual populations, most especially a people group's religion and religious customs.

---

[11] Leif Gunnar Engedal, "*Homo Viator*. The Search for Identity and Authentic Spirituality in a Post-modern Context," in Kirsi Tirri (ed.) *Religion, Spirituality and Identity* (Bern: Peter Lang, 2006), 45-64, 58.
[12] Ivan Varga, "Detraditionalization and Retraditionalization," in Mark Juergensmeyer and Wade Clark Roof (eds.), *Encyclopedia of Global Religion* (Los Angeles: Sage Publications, 2012), 295-98, 297.

Globalization is thus provoking a very real sense of cultural insecurity among the world's national populations, and as a result, they are increasingly striking back, largely through this process known as retraditionalization, where more and more populations are re-asserting their customs, cultures, and traditions as mechanisms of resistance against globalization's anti-cultural and anti-traditional dynamics. It thus appears that we are seeing a very clear case of that here with the Yellow Vest Uprising and its adoption of Christian symbolism as a form of unity and solidarity.

The yellow vest symbolizes the grievances of the working class so callously displaced and dismissed by the gentrified processes of globalization and its economic elite. They've seen their industrial jobs shipped overseas by trade policies that seek to keep production costs low so as to guard against inflation. This dominant monetary policy of virtually all Western globalist nations has not only contributed to the inordinate unemployment in rural areas but has also kept wages completely stagnant over the last 20 years. The yellow vest signifies that globalism is broken; it's not working for a massive portion of the global population, and while globalism is certainly making our political, economic, educational, and media elites very, very rich, it is doing so at the expense of those who've loved and sacrificed for their nation, their people, their cultures and customs for generations. The yellow vest is truly a very powerful symbol that is indeed catching the intention of the entire world and will do so long after the movement inevitably ends. In short, when the history books are written, the yellow vest will be seen as nothing less than one of the most powerful protest symbols in history.

CHAPTER THREE

Macron's Faustian Bargain

With his political career in peril and the future of globalist Europe in doubt, the French President Emmanuel Macron tried to quell the Yellow Vest Uprising in a televised address to the French nation. By the time of the address, numbers had swelled to well over 100,000 protestors, and it was clear that Macron simply couldn't avoid the national implications that such protests had for his political future. The networks aired his pre-taped address that differed dramatically from his original dismissal of the demonstrators a few weeks back when he referred to them as "thugs." But since then, over the course of four weeks, the uprising had grown to proportions that Macron could not have imagined in his worst nightmares. And now, his political career was in jeopardy.

And so, Macron got on television and encouraged companies to give their workers bonuses while promising to enact tax reductions. He pledged that he would raise the minimum wage and abolish taxes on overtime pay starting January first, and also promised to scrap a tax hike on pensioners; significant concessions, no doubt, and a number of the demonstrators voiced their support for reforms such as these.

And yet, given that Macron had absolutely no intention of slowing down the globalist enterprise that he has planned for France and the whole of Europe, these measures were interpreted as little more than an attempt at buying off the protestors, and, in effect shutting these 'thugs' up. Said differently, many interpreted the televised address as little more than Macron's attempt to buy his political future back.

Macron appeared to be making the same kind of mistake that so many analysts continue to make when it comes to populist movements. He and others believe that this societal unrest can be resolved solely through *economic* means. Pay the people off, they go home happy, and the whole thing is done. But that is emphatically not what is going on here, certainly not in France nor the wider continent. Globalist leaders are sorely mistaken if they think that they can reduce the cause of social unrest to mere economic factors.

What Macron and his ilk do not get is that the nationalist populist uprisings currently going on in Europe began long before the 2008 economic crisis. Eatwell and Goodwin document how populist movements enjoyed their greatest successes in nations that were already experiencing rather strong economic growth long before 2008.[13] For example, in

---

[13] Eatwell and Goodwin, *National Populism*, 5-8.

Britain, Nigel Farage and his self-proclaimed People's Army first stormed the political stage in the European parliament elections back in 2004, and this was just after 48 consecutive periods of economic growth, drawing tremendous support from rather affluent conservatives. And in terms of the working class, one study found that before the 2008 economic crisis, working-class voters were twice as likely as their middle-class counterparts to vote for national populists in Austria, three times as likely in Belgium and France, and four times as likely in Norway. And that's precisely what we saw when it came to the last presidential election in France. Marine Le Pen won an overwhelming majority in a single electoral demographic and that was the working class, the very people who are donning yellow vests throughout the entire nation of France.[14] In other words, though workers made up about half of the electorate, they delivered two-thirds of their votes to the national populists, particularly in France.

This is emphatically *not* merely an economic issue that Macron can throw a few Euros at and think it will all go away. At the heart of this Yellow Vest Uprising is this growing sense that the elites in charge of our political, economic, media, and educational institutions operate and govern according to their own interests rather than the interests of the common people, the populace. And when they try to make their voices heard, these protestors simply feel like no one among the elite is listening to them. They

---

[14] Ibid, 24.

certainly do not feel listened to by their politicians, but neither do they feel like they are being represented by the elite, corporatist, globalist media who seem to care about a whole host of issues that have nothing whatsoever to do with the concerns of the average Frenchmen. When asked the question by pollsters, 'Do you believe that your politicians do not care about you or your concerns?', 78 percent of French responders agreed with that statement.[15] Nearly 80 percent of French believe that their politicians do not care about them or their concerns. This is not about economics; this is fundamentally about a deeply rooted sense of disenfranchisement from the political conversation that more and more people feel they have been excluded from.

And one of the reasons for this is that both France and Europe's elite want to foster multicultural societies within their respective nations, even though the vast majority of populations want nothing to do with that. And again, the studies are absolutely conclusive: 95 percent of Dutch, Brits, Hungarians, Germans, Greeks, Poles, and French believe that it is either very or somewhat important that people speak the official language of their nation.[16] Over 80 percent of French believe that sharing their nation's cultural heritage is important to being part of the national community; note how this so starkly contrasts with migrant and predominantly Muslim enclaves that are formed

---

[15] Ibid, 123.
[16] Ibid, 157.

throughout their cities and their various regions. If you are going to be a permanent part of France, then 80 percent of French believe you need to be accustomed to their language and cultural heritage.

All of this is, of course, not to say that there are not real economic issues that need to be dealt with; that is for sure. Again, these protestors are disproportionately the victims of globalization's worldwide division of labor, where manufacturing and industrial factory jobs are shipped out to third world nations while capital and finance are relocated to urban centers, and this process has left rural populations highly unemployed; and that's a lot of what's going on here. You have French citizens who do not have the money to live in Paris but who cannot work in their rural areas because of the high unemployment that came about as the result of this global division of labor; and so, they have to commute to the cities to work. Then the government turns around and levies all these gas taxes on them in the process! It is ridiculous. They already blame their government for having shipped their manufacturing and industry jobs overseas to third world countries; now that same government wants to impose a fuel tax on the very people who have to drive cars into the cities because the government shipped off their rural jobs. You can see why so many have had it!

But the whole notion that the whole of the Yellow Vests concerns can be reduced to the economic, that all you have to do is throw some Euros at the problem and think you have solved it, as Macron did in his speech, is just further proof of how far removed he and others are from the basic concerns of so much of the French population. Macron really is a globalist; he really could care less about how people are disaffected by all of his globalist reforms; he really does appear to have the attitude: 'Let them drive Teslas' and be done with it. I see no evidence that he actually understands the massive tectonic shift that is been underway for several years now, long before any major economic crisis.

And so, Macron's concessions were all too little too late. Europe is changing right from under his feet. And these tectonic shifts are in many ways just getting started. Macron may have thought he could buy his way out of this; that he could buy back his political future, but in reality, as it turns out, the future belongs to the populists.

CHAPTER FOUR

How the Yellow Vests are Changing France

As the Yellow Vest Uprising entered into Act 16 or its fourth straight month in existence, there seemed little question as to *whether* the protests had transformed France; the question was more: *how* and *in what ways* was France changing as a result of these demonstrations?

Let's start first with French President Emmanuel Macron himself. Before the Yellow Vest Uprising, Macron was considered by both pundits and politicians alike to be the new de facto leader of the European Union. Merkel has been dwindling into irrelevance as her political clout has begun to wane. Macron appeared to revel in this role as the default leader of Europe at the 100th commemoration of the end of World War I, where he arrogated to himself the role of admonishing Presidents Trump and Vladimir Putin on the dangers of nationalism and virtues of globalism. That was Macron before Paris began to burn.

Since the Yellow Vest Uprising, his approval ratings have tanked to barely 18 percent and, he has faced a no-confidence vote in the French Parliament. He has actually admitted to humiliating France and the French people throughout these protests. France has lost billions of dollars in tourist revenue. And Macron has basically dropped the 'leader of Europe' rhetoric. For example, when was the last time he spoke of the need to assemble a European army? I think the first and major effect that the Yellow Vest Uprising has had is that it has utterly humiliated the French president and has completely paralyzed his political leverage over France and the wider continent.

The second change that the Yellow Vest Uprising has brought about is that it has foregrounded the concerns of the middle-class and lower-middle-class people that the media has largely ignored. These are the very concerns that compelled millions of people to vote for Brexit in Britain and, of course, for Donald Trump in the States. But the elites in the media tend to ignore the actual reasons behind these victories in favor of a bunch of escapist concoctions that fault the Brits for not actually knowing what they were voting for, or how Americans were swayed by fake news spread by Russian bots on social media.

But what the legacy media is finally giving some attention to – as a result of these protests – is that globalization has indeed created what we called above a 'global division of labor,' where manufacturing and industrial factory jobs are shipped out to third world nations while capital and finance are relocated to urban centers, a process that has left rural populations highly unemployed. And so, scholar Christopher Guilluy has pointed to the growth of what he calls 'peripheral France,' which is made up of people who can't live in urban centers but who can't necessarily find jobs in rural areas; so they more and more feel like they've been completely shut out from the national conversation and decision making.[17] And to make matters even worse, between the years of 2004 and 2013, France spent nearly 40 billion Euros to refurbish and rebuild mainly ethnic-minority housing centers through-out their cities, but they didn't do anything even remotely like this on similarly depressed areas inhabited by native French citizens.

A third way the Yellow Vest Uprising is changing France is that it has effectively taken over and is now driving the national conversation. This was an observation made by a writer over at *The Atlantic,* who sees actually what is being billed as the 'Great Debate' that was initiated by President Macron as a rather stunning development bearing witness to just how much the Yellow Vest Uprising is changing the tenor of French politics.[18] Macron, of course, is doing

---

[17]https://www.irishtimes.com/culture/books/twilight-of-the-elites-review-an-insight-into-france-s-gilets-jaunes-1.3817848.
[18]https://www.theatlantic.com/international/archive/2019/01/macron-grand-debate-yellow-vests/580810/.

everything he can to limit the debate to those things he wants to talk about and has made it rather clear that he has no intention of deviating from his globalist-inspired reforms in France. But there is also no question that both Macron and those globalist-inspired reforms are provoking enormous blowback, and the 'Grand Debate' serves now as a wider platform for the expression of just such a national backlash. Macron has been forced to consider a number of tax cuts as well as scrap the fuel tax that served as the impetus for the Uprising.[19]

A fourth way the Yellow Vest Uprising is changing France is that it is reinvigorating and, in many ways, redefining the French political right. One of the things that commentators are not taking into consideration when they say that the Yellow Vest movement is beginning to dwindle is the number of conservative political and cultural movements and organizations that are beginning to find extraordinary solidarity with the Yellow Vest Uprising, and are indeed beginning the process of formally uniting themselves with that uprising. As we'll develop below, this is why commentators are indeed noticing that the Yellow Vest Uprising is giving rise to what is being called the 'New French Right,' which raises the question: to what extent is this renewal going to propel parties like Marine Le Pen's National Rally to victory in the upcoming European Parliament elections at the end of May? If Le Pen's National Rally absolutely storms into Brussels by virtue of those elections, you can be sure that

---

[19] https://www.bbc.com/news/world-europe-47859485.

pundits will be admitting that the Yellow Vest Uprising had a direct effect on the very make-up, not just of the politics in France but indeed the politics of the wider European Union.

These are just some observations on how the Yellow Vest Uprising is indeed changing France. It is, simply put, one of the most astonishing political movements to arise within the French nation in the last century, and in many ways promises to challenge globalization and change their nation – and perhaps even the continent – in ways that none of us, a mere few months ago, could have ever foreseen.

CHAPTER FIVE

Yellow Vest Uprising and the Dawn of the New French Right

As protests continued to rage across France in cities such as Clermont-Ferrand and the northern city of Rennes in Brittany, Epinal in the northeast, Bordeaux and Strasbourg and, of course, Paris, the epicenter of the protests, the French government began to turn on Macron. It was not just the conservative opposition, which is not necessarily a fan of these protests; the center-right likes these protests only as long as it is politically damaging to President Macron. But if the center-right came to power, they would be instituting very similar pro-globalist economic policies as well. Nevertheless, the conservative opposition has consistently blamed Macron for letting the Yellow Vest Uprising spiral out of control. These critiques can't be chalked up to mere politics. Macron has been rightly faulted for a series of missteps that has only served to exacerbate the whole situation. He's publicly smeared the protestors, calling them 'thugs,' anti-Semites, and homophobes; he has tried to buy them off with tax-cuts and wage increases; at one point, he even claimed that he (Macron!) was a Yellow Vester in that he shared their same concerns. So, Macron certainly has not helped himself in all of this.

As far as the political left is concerned, Macron is to be faulted for causing a massive surge in a renewed nationalist populist right. The political left recognizes that Macron right now is really no political match for the rather popular figures such as Italy's Matteo Salvini and Hungary's Viktor Orban, both of whom have been taunting Macron as a failed globalist leader who cannot even please his own citizens. If Macron cannot even serve rightly his own citizens, what on earth business does he have lecturing the rest of Europe on how they should conduct themselves? Where does a guy who is overseeing months of non-stop mass nationwide protests come off lecturing Europeans about a continental army?

But more than that, commentators and pundits are recognizing that while the Yellow Vest Uprising has intentionally not allied itself with any particular political movement, it does appear that they are attracting a number of cultural movements and organizations in an extraordinary show of solidarity; movements and organizations that are beginning the process of formally uniting themselves with the Yellow Vests, and in so doing, are emerging into a New French Right.

For example, Quarz.com is reporting that a number of traditional conservative Catholic movements such as France's pro-life movement have been reinvigorated by the Yellow Vest uprising.[20] These social conservatives are noticing that they, like the yellow vests, have been shut out of the democratic process. Their argument is that Macron's government has repeatedly stated that it will not even consider discussing issues such as abortion and same-sex marriage rights as part of this so-called 'Grand Debate' that the government launched in January of 2019. In other words, social conservatives see that the crisis of the Yellow Vests is a crisis in democracy, and they are welcoming the Yellow Vests to the periphery of democratic involvement to which social conservatives have thus far been consigned.

What we are beginning to see now is a union between French Catholic conservatives and the populist Yellow Vest Uprising. This union of religious conservatives and a populist blue-collar anti-globalist movement has been in the making for some time now. According to the political scientist and historian, Mark Lilla, it is part of the emergence of what he calls "the new French right."[21] The new French right, according to Lilla, is a young, right-wing intellectual elite who are not just socially conservative but are also economic nationalists. They reject the whole notion of "unregulated global financial markets, neoliberal austerity, and consumerism." They despise Facebook and Google and other Big Tech tyrants, and they are, of course,

---

[20] https://qz.com/1529384/the-yellow-vest-movement-is-giving-frances-social-conservatives-a-new-platform/.
[21] https://www.nybooks.com/articles/2018/12/20/two-roads-for-the-new-french-right/.

virulently anti-EU and anti-unfettered immigration. In short, Lilla has discovered that the new right is the nationalist, populist, and traditionalist right.[22] The new right is made up of conservative French Catholics, traditionalists, who are not just outbreeding their secular globalist counterparts (30 percent of French women have over 50 percent of the children!); they are standing arm-in-arm with rural blue-collar workers who have seen their factory and industrial jobs shipped overseas because of the economic and trade policies of urban-based cosmopolitan globalists. They are aligning their social conservativism with pro-blue-collar economic nationalism and protectionism.

What is so interesting here is that both the French cultural conservatives and the Yellow Vest protestors are absolutely united in the conviction that the solutions to their economic and cultural predicaments can no longer be found in the current globalist structures and its political and economic representatives. The current globalist order, either in its politically-left manifestation or its politically-right manifestation, is simply no longer capable of resolving the problems as seen through the lens of France's social conservatives and rural populists. For example, they recognize that the Republicans of the center-right have long ago made their peace with globalization and have left all matters of social

---

[22] For a more detailed development of the new right, see my *The New Nationalism: How the Populist Right is Defeating Globalism and Awakening a New Political Order* (Newark, DE: Turley Talks Publishing), 2018.

morality a matter of mere private and personal choice. In the same way, the center-left parties like Macron's En Marche have embraced globalization even further and have made it their mission to enforce punitive taxes upon their population so as to comply with extreme environmental regulations. Neither the center-left or center-right has anything to offer France's cultural conservatives and blue-collar workers.

This is why the combination of France's cultural conservatives and the Yellow Vest Uprising is such an existential threat to the globalist world order. What makes the emerging coalition between French cultural conservatives and the Yellow Vest protestors so dangerous to the current world order is that their absolutely unrelenting demands find virtually no possible solution within the given globalist structures and its representative elite.

Now as Mark Lilla notes, one of the key leaders that are emerging from this coalition of the new right is Marion Maréchal, who is the granddaughter of National Front founder, Jean-Marie Le Pen and the niece of Marine Le Pen. Marion used to be difficult to place ideologically. She was more socially conservative than the National Front leadership but more neoliberal in her economics. What is so fascinating is that that has changed. Right around this time last year, she gave a monumental speech at CPAC, the Conservative Political Action Committee in Washington, DC, where she outlined her vision for how a coalition of social conservatives on the one hand and blue-collar workers on the other were going to take back the nation of France.

And she is not talking just about politics. She is talking about taking back the culture. One of the things she has done since the speech in Washington DC is that she has opened a private graduate school in Lyon, the Institute of Social, Economic, and Political Sciences, with the aim, according to Marion, of displacing the culture that dominates our "nomadic, globalized, deracinated liberal system." And Lilla points out that it is basically a business school but with great books courses in philosophy, literature, history, and rhetoric, as well as practical ones on management and "political and cultural combat."

So, given that Marion is still in her 20s, all of this says that it does appear we really are seeing the rise of a new French right that may indeed be nothing less than the dominant political and cultural future of France.

CHAPTER SIX

Macron's Crisis and the Prospect of a Nationalist Takeover of Europe

Journalists and pundits hardly limit the fallout from the Yellow Vest Uprising to French politics. Note the following headlines: from *The Guardian*: "Macron's Crisis in France is a Danger to all of Europe;" here's one from *Bloomberg*: "History to Macron: French Protesters Always Win;" the *International*: "Macron, What Now? France Faces Worst Social Unrest Since 1968;" and from *Politico*: "The Rise and Fall of Macron's European Revolution." Even the ultra-liberal Slate Magazine had this for a headline: "France's Latest Protests are a Rejection of All Things Macron;" or perhaps my favorite, this from *The Local France*: "What the yellow vests now want is Macron on his knees."

In the midst of all of these headlines is a reluctant admission by many in the corporatist globalist media: the fall of Macron means ultimately nothing less than the fall of their vision of a globalist Europe. They can't help but just marvel, in almost shocked silence, how literally just days after Macron publicly denounced nationalism in his public rebuke of President Trump at the World War I centennial comme- moration, France began to literally crumble under the weight of the rise of populist and nationalist sentiments. Those who believed and 'reported' on the inevitability of a globalist world order, an unstoppable inexorable end to history, were now choking on the fumes from a slew of burning cars in Paris.

Read past the headlines and into some of these stories, and you'll realize just how much the globalist media elite recognize that their days may, in fact, be numbered. They can hear it in the sneers and jesting laughter coming from the likes of Italy's Matteo Salvini who taunted Macron by saying that *he* was France's biggest problem, not the protesters. President Trump has, of course, piled on; he tweeted out that he was glad to see Macron finally come to the same conclusion he came to over two years ago about the Paris Agreement and the inordinate cost of living increases that such an Agreement would force on their respective populations.

But mockery aside, media pundits are recognizing that this kind of social instability surrounding Macron, who, since the demise of Angela Merkel, had become the symbol of the globalist vision of Europe, can only mean disaster in the upcoming European parliament elections in May. It was just a couple of months back that Macron publicly proclaimed himself as the arch-enemy of Salvini and Hungary's Viktor

Orban. *The Telegraph* reported that Orban issued a behind the scenes provocation against the French president, saying that the upcoming elections in the European parliament in May basically boils down to a duel between him and Macron.[23] The election was coming down to nationalism vs. globalism, and Orban asserted that his nationalist vision for Europe was going to win big time and that Macron's globalism was going down to defeat. And Macron came out and responded that he wasn't going to give an inch to nationalists and their hate speech, which, if true, was a rather embarrassingly inept reply.

As it turns out, Orban appears to have been rather prophetic, not knowing the eventual Yellow Vest Uprising would lend such credence to his prognostication. Indeed, Macron has been willing to give plenty of ground to nationalist populists who want to take their country back from globalist elitists who govern and operate with values and visions completely at odds from the vast majority of their own citizens. Just months after his reported altercation with the nationalist Orban, Macron, the supposed globalist savior of Europe, looked absolutely and completely paralyzed, and as one liberal globalist pundit put it, it appears that "the last rites could soon be read over his European plans."[24]

---

[23]https://www.telegraph.co.uk/news/2018/09/16/hungarys-orban-issued-personal-challenge-macron-telling-populist/.
[24]https://www.theguardian.com/commentisfree/2018/dec/04/emmanuel-macron-crisis-france-europe-far-right.

Pundits are recognizing that a weakened Macron will now only fuel and intensify the nationalist populist movement throughout the entire European continent. The Le Pens, the Orbans, and the Salvinis are all waiting in the wings, ready to make the next EU election in France a referendum against the elitist rule of Macron. We ought not to forget that Italy, too, had some pretty massive protest marches a few years back, led by the comedian and founder of the populist Five Star Movement, Beppe Grillo. The protests were called the 'vaffanculo' demonstrations, which translates into the 'f*** you' demonstrations; within just a matter of months after the march, the populist Five Star Movement, along with the nationalist Italian League, was swept into power forming the first official nationalist populist majority government in the West. With these protests throughout France continuing well into their fifth month with no end in sight, it appears certain that the West's newest nationalist populist government will not be its last. The Yellow Vest Uprising is providing its own prophetic contribution: it does appear that the nationalist populist right is indeed poised to conquer Europe.

Thank you again for purchasing this book!

I hope this book gave you a fresh understanding of the political, economic, and cultural trends behind the Yellow Vest Uprising and what those trends mean for the future of France and the whole of Europe.

If you enjoyed this book, then I'd like to ask you for a favor: Would you be kind enough to leave a review for this book on Amazon? I would so greatly appreciate it!

Thank you so much, and may God richly bless you!

Steve Turley

www.turleytalks.com

Check Out My Other Books

Below you'll find some of my other popular books that are popular on Amazon. Simply go to the links below to check them out. Alternatively, you can visit my author page on Amazon to see my other works.

- *The Abolition of Sanity: C.S. Lewis on the Consequences of Modernism* https://amzn.to/2IAlGkg

- *The Return of Christendom: Demography, Politics, and the Coming Christian Majority* https://amzn.to/2VM2W4O

- *The New Nationalism: How the Populist Right is Defeating Globalism and Awakening a New Political Order* https://amzn.to/2WEP11u

- *The Triumph of Tradition: How the Resurgence of Religion is Reawakening a Conservative World* https://amzn.to/2xieNO3

- *Classical vs. Modern Education: A Vision from C.S. Lewis* http://amzn.to/2opDZju

- *President Trump and Our Post-Secular Future:
  How the 2016 Election Signals the Dawning of a
  Conservative Nationalist Age*
  http://amzn.to/2B87Q22

- *Gazing: Encountering the Mystery of Art*
  https://amzn.to/2yKi6k9

- *Beauty Matters: Creating a High Aesthetic in School
  Culture* https://amzn.to/2L8Ejd7

- *Ever After: How to Overcome Cynical Students with
  the Role of Wonder in Education*
  http://amzn.to/2jbJI78

- *Movies and the Moral Imagination: Finding Paradise
  in Films* http://amzn.to/2zjghJj

- *Echoes of Eternity: A Classical Guide to Music*
  https://amzn.to/2O0bYrY

- *Health Care Sharing Ministries: How Christians are
  Revolutionizing Medical Cost and Care*
  http://amzn.to/2B2Q8B2

- *The Face of Infinite of Love: Athanasius on the
  Incarnation* http://amzn.to/2oxULNM

- *Stressed Out: Learn How an Ancient Christian Practice Can Relieve Stress and Overcome Anxiety* http://amzn.to/2kFzcpc

- *Wise Choice: Six Steps to Godly Decision Making* http://amzn.to/2qy3C2Z

- *Awakening Wonder: A Classical Guide to Truth, Goodness, and Beauty* http://amzn.to/2ziKR5H

- *Worldview Guide for* A Christmas Carol http://amzn.to/2BCcKHO

- *The Ritualized Revelation of the Messianic Age: Washings and Meals in Galatians and 1 Corinthians* http://amzn.to/2B0mGvf

If the links do not work, for whatever reason, you can simply search for these titles on the Amazon website to find them.

About www.TurleyTalks.com

Are we seeing the revitalization of Christian civilization?

For decades, the world has been dominated by a process known as globalization, an economic and political system that hollows out and erodes a culture's traditions, customs, and religions, all the while conditioning populations to rely on the expertise of a tiny class of technocrats for every aspect of their social and economic lives.

Until now.

All over the world, there's been a massive blowback against the anti-cultural processes of globalization and its secular aristocracy. From Russia to Europe and now in the U.S., citizens are rising up and reasserting their religion, culture, and nation as mechanisms of resistance against the dehumanizing tendencies of secularism and globalism.

And it's just the beginning.

The secular world is at its brink, and a new traditionalist age is rising.

Join me each week as we examine these worldwide trends, discover answers to today's toughest challenges, and together learn to live in the present in light of even better things to come.

So hop on over to www.TurleyTalks.com and have a look around. Make sure to sign-up for our weekly Email Newsletter where you'll get lots of free giveaways, private Q&As, and tons of great content. Check out our YouTube channel (www.youtube.com/c/DrSteveTurley) where you'll understand current events in light of conservative trends to help you flourish in your personal and professional life. And of course, 'Like' us on Facebook and follow us on Twitter.

Thank you so much for your support and for your part in this cultural renewal.

About the Author

Steve Turley (PhD, Durham University) is an internationally recognized scholar, speaker, and classical guitarist. He is the author of over a dozen books, including *Classical vs. Modern Education: A Vision from C.S. Lewis, Awakening Wonder: A Classical Guide to Truth, Goodness, and Beauty*, and *The Ritualized Revelation of the Messianic Age: Washings and Meals in Galatians and 1 Corinthians*. Steve's popular YouTube channel showcases weekly his expertise in the rise of nationalism, populism, and traditionalism throughout the world, and his podcasts and writings on civilization, society, culture, education, and the arts are widely accessed at TurleyTalks.com. He is a faculty member at Tall Oaks Classical School in Bear, DE, where he teaches Theology and Rhetoric, and was formerly Professor of Fine Arts at Eastern University. Steve lectures at universities, conferences, and churches throughout the U.S. and abroad. His research and writings have appeared in such journals as *Christianity and Literature, Calvin Theological Journal, First Things, Touchstone*, and *The Chesterton Review*. He and his wife, Akiko, have four children and live in Newark, DE, where they together enjoy fishing, gardening, and watching *Duck Dynasty* marathons.

Made in the USA
Monee, IL
30 October 2021

80354014R00033